I0484710

BUSINESS

LEADERSHIP

:: Author ::

ASHOKKUMAR D. PATEL

(M.COM., SLET)

PUBLISHED BY

Hemchadracharya International Publishing House
HQ. At & Po. Chaveli., Ta- Chansma,
Dist- Patan, North Gujarat, India, Asia.
www.iphouseindia.com

BUSINESS LEADERSHIP

First Publication: 17TH DECEMBER, 2014

Copyright: Author

(c) ASHOKKUMAR D. PATEL

ISBN:- 978-15-08675-60-0

Price: Rs.750/- INDIA

$ 15 OUTSIDE INDIA

PUBLISHED BY

Hemchadracharya International Publishing House
HQ. At & Po. Chaveli., Ta- Chansma,
Dist- Patan, North Gujarat, India, Asia.
www.iphouseindia.com

*Dedicated
to
my
Parents*

❖ **Leadership Basics**

❖ **What is Leadership**

Leadership is a process by which an executive can direct, guide and influence the behavior and work of others towards accomplishment of specific goals in a given situation. Leadership is the ability of a manager to induce the subordinates to work with confidence and zeal.

Leadership is the potential to influence behaviour of others. It is also defined as the capacity to influence a group towards the realization of a goal. Leaders are required to develop future visions, and to motivate the organizational members to want to achieve the visions.

According to Keith Davis, "Leadership is the ability to persuade others to seek defined objectives enthusiastically. It is the human factor which binds a group together and motivates it towards goals."

❖ **Characteristics of Leadership**

It is a inter-personal process in which a manager is into influencing and guiding workers towards attainment of goals.

1. It denotes a few qualities to be present in a person which includes intelligence, maturity and personality.

2. It is a group process. It involves two or more people interacting with each other.

3. A leader is involved in shaping and moulding the behaviour of the group towards accomplishment of organizational goals.

4. Leadership is situation bound. There is no best style of leadership. It all depends upon tackling with the situations.

❖ Importance of Leadership

Leadership is an important function of management which helps to maximize efficiency and to achieve organizational goals. The following points justify the importance of leadership in a concern.

1. **Initiates action-** Leader is a person who starts the work by communicating the policies and plans to the subordinates from where the work actually starts.

2. **Motivation-** A leader proves to be playing an incentive role in the concern's working. He motivates the employees with economic and non-economic rewards and thereby gets the work from the subordinates.

3. **Providing guidance-** A leader has to not only supervise but also play a guiding role for the subordinates. Guidance here means instructing the subordinates the

way they have to perform their work effectively and efficiently.

4. **Creating confidence-** Confidence is an important factor which can be achieved through expressing the work efforts to the subordinates, explaining them clearly their role and giving them guidelines to achieve the goals effectively. It is also important to hear the employees with regards to their complaints and problems.

5. **Building morale-** Morale denotes willing co-operation of the employees towards their work and getting them into confidence and winning their trust. A leader can be a morale booster by achieving full co-operation so that they perform with best of their abilities as they work to achieve goals.

6. **Builds work environment-** Management is getting things done from people. An efficient work environment helps in sound and stable growth. Therefore, human relations should be kept into mind by a leader. He should have personal contacts with employees and should listen to their problems and solve them. He should treat employees on humanitarian terms.

7. **Co-ordination-** Co-ordination can be achieved through reconciling personal interests with organizational goals. This synchronization can be achieved through proper and effective co-ordination which should be primary motive of a leader.

❖ Role of a Leader

Following are the main roles of a leader in an organization :

1. **Required at all levels-** Leadership is a function which is important at all <u>levels of management</u>. In the top level, it is important for getting co-operation in formulation of plans and policies. In the middle and lower level, it is required for interpretation and execution of plans and programmes framed by the top management. Leadership can be exercised through guidance and counseling of the subordinates at the time of execution of plans.

2. **Representative of the organization-** A leader, i.e., a manager is said to be the representative of the enterprise. He has to represent the concern at seminars, conferences, general meetings, etc. His role is to communicate the rationale of the enterprise to outside public. He is also representative of the own department which he leads.

3. **Integrates and reconciles the personal goals with organizational goals-** A leader through leadership traits helps in reconciling/ integrating the personal goals of the employees with the organizational goals. He is trying to co-ordinate the efforts of people towards a common purpose and thereby achieves objectives. This can be done only if he can influence and get willing co-operation and urge to accomplish the objectives

4. **He solicits support-** A leader is a manager and besides that he is a person who entertains and invites support and co- operation of subordinates. This he can do by his personality, intelligence, maturity and experience which can provide him positive result. In this regard, a leader has to invite suggestions and if possible implement them into plans and programmes of enterprise. This way, he can solicit full support of employees which results in willingness to work and thereby effectiveness in running of a concern.

5. **As a friend, philosopher and guide-** A leader must possess the three dimensional traits in him. He can be a friend by sharing the feelings, opinions and desires with the employees. He can be a philosopher by utilizing his intelligence and experience and thereby guiding the employees as and when time requires. He can be a guide by supervising and communicating the employees the plans and policies of top management and secure their co-operation to achieve the goals of a concern. At times he can also play the role of a counselor by counseling and a problem-solving approach. He can listen to the problems of the employees and try to solve them.

- **Qualities of a Leader**

A leader has got multidimensional traits in him which makes

him appealing and effective in behavior. The following are the requisites to be present in a good leader:

1. **Physical appearance-** A leader must have a pleasing appearance. Physique and health are very important for a good leader.

2. **Vision and foresight-** A leader cannot maintain influence unless he exhibits that he is forward looking. He has to visualize situations and thereby has to frame logical programmes.

3. **Intelligence-** A leader should be intelligent enough to examine problems and difficult situations. He should be analytical who weighs pros and cons and then summarizes the situation. Therefore, a positive bent of mind and mature outlook is very important.

4. **Communicative skills-** A leader must be able to communicate the policies and procedures clearly, precisely and effectively. This can be helpful in persuasion and stimulation.

5. **Objective-** A leader has to be having a fair outlook which is free from bias and which does not reflects his willingness towards a particular individual. He should develop his own opinion and should base his judgement on facts and logic.

6. **Knowledge of work-** A leader should be very precisely knowing the nature of work of his subordinates because

it is then he can win the trust and confidence of his subordinates.

7. **Sense of responsibility-** Responsibility and accountability towards an individual's work is very important to bring a sense of influence. A leader must have a sense of responsibility towards organizational goals because only then he can get maximum of capabilities exploited in a real sense. For this, he has to motivate himself and arouse and urge to give best of his abilities. Only then he can motivate the subordinates to the best.

8. **Self-confidence and will-power-** Confidence in himself is important to earn the confidence of the subordinates. He should be trustworthy and should handle the situations with full will power. (You can read more about Self-Confidence at : <u>Self Confidence - Tips to be Confident and Eliminate Your Apprehensions</u>).

9. **Humanist-**This trait to be present in a leader is essential because he deals with human beings and is in personal contact with them. He has to handle the personal problems of his subordinates with great care and attention. Therefore, treating the human beings on humanitarian grounds is essential for building a congenial environment.

10. **Empathy-** It is an old adage "Stepping into the shoes of others". This is very important because fair judgement

and objectivity comes only then. A leader should understand the problems and complaints of employees and should also have a complete view of the needs and aspirations of the employees. This helps in improving human relations and personal contacts with the employees.

From the above qualities present in a leader, one can understand the scope of leadership and it's importance for scope of business. A leader cannot have all traits at one time. But a few of them helps in achieving effective results.

- **Leadership and Management - Relationship & Differences**

Leadership and management are the terms that are often considered synonymous. It is essential to understand that leadership is an essential part of effective management. As a crucial component of management, remarkable leadership behaviour stresses upon building an environment in which each and every employee develops and excels. Leadership is defined as the potential to influence and drive the group efforts towards the accomplishment of goals. This influence may originate from formal sources, such as that provided by acquisition of managerial position in an organization.

A manager must have traits of a leader, i.e., he must

possess leadership qualities. Leaders develop and begin strategies that build and sustain competitive advantage. Organizations require robust leadership and robust management for optimal organizational efficiency.

- **Differences between Leadership and Management**

Leadership differs from management in a sense that:

1. While managers lay down the structure and delegates authority and responsibility, leaders provides direction by developing the organizational vision and communicating it to the employees and inspiring them to achieve it.
2. While management includes focus on planning, organizing, staffing, directing and controlling; leadership is mainly a part of directing function of management. Leaders focus on listening, building relationships, teamwork, inspiring, motivating and persuading the followers.
3. While a leader gets his authority from his followers, a manager gets his authority by virtue of his position in the organization.
4. While managers follow the organization's policies and procedure, the leaders follow their own instinct.
5. Management is more of science as the managers are exact, planned, standard, logical and more of mind. Leadership, on the other hand, is an art. In an

organization, if the managers are required, then leaders are a must/essential.

6. While management deals with the technical dimension in an organization or the job content; leadership deals with the people aspect in an organization.

7. While management measures/evaluates people by their name, past records, present performance; leadership sees and evaluates individuals as having potential for things that can't be measured, i.e., it deals with future and the performance of people if their potential is fully extracted.

8. If management is reactive, leadership is proactive.

9. Management is based more on written communication, while leadership is based more on verbal communication.

The organizations which are over managed and under-led do not perform up to the benchmark. Leadership accompanied by management sets a new direction and makes efficient use of resources to achieve it. Both leadership and management are essential for individual as well as organizational success.

- **Leader versus Manager**

"Leadership and managership are two synonymous terms" is an incorrect statement. Leadership doesn't require any managerial position to act as a leader. On the other hand, a manager can be a true manager only if he has got the traits of leader in him. By virtue of his position, manager has to provide leadership to his group. A manager has to perform all five functions to achieve goals, i.e., <u>Planning</u>, <u>Organizing</u>, Staffing, <u>Directing</u>, and Controlling. Leadership is a part of these functions. Leadership as a general term is not related to managership. A person can be a leader by virtue of qualities in him. For example: leader of a club, class, welfare association, social organization, etc. Therefore, it is true to say that, "All managers are leaders, but all leaders are not managers."

A leader is one who influences the behavior and work of others in group efforts towards achievement of specified goals in a given situation. On the other hand, manager can be a true manager only if he has got traits of leader in him. Manager at all levels are expected to be the leaders of work groups so that subordinates willingly carry instructions and accept their guidance. A person can be a leader by virtue of all qualities in him.

Leaders and Managers can be compared on the following basis:

Basis	Manager	Leader
Origin	A person becomes a manager by virtue of his position.	A person becomes a leader on basis of his personal qualities.

Formal Rights	Manager has got formal rights in an organization because of his status.	Rights are not available to a leader.
Followers	The subordinates are the followers of managers.	The group of employees whom the leaders leads are his followers.
Functions	A manager performs all five functions of management.	Leader influences people to work willingly for group objectives.
Necessity	A manager is very essential to a concern.	A leader is required to create cordial relation between person working in and for organization.
Stability	It is more stable.	Leadership is temporary.
Mutual Relationship	All managers are leaders.	All leaders are not managers.
Accountability	Manager is	Leaders have no well

	accountable for self and subordinates behaviour and performance.	defined accountability.
Concern	A manager's concern is organizational goals.	A leader's concern is group goals and member's satisfaction.
Followers	People follow manager by virtue of job description.	People follow them on voluntary basis.
Role continuation	A manager can continue in office till he performs his duties satisfactorily in congruence with organizational goals.	A leader can maintain his position only through day to day wishes of followers.
Sanctions	Manager has command over allocation and distribution of sanctions.	A leader has command over different sanctions and related task records. These sanctions are

		essentially of informal nature.

• Authority vs Leadership

The authority exercised is a kind of legitimate power and people follow figures exercising it, because their positions demand so irrespective of the person holding the position. Leaders in organizations and elsewhere may have formal authorities but they mostly rely on the informal authority that they exercise on people to influence them. Leaders are trusted for their judgment and respected for their expertise, integrity etc and hence followed and not because they hold a certain position. For e.g. M.K. Gandhi for most part did not hold any official position to lead the Indian freedom struggle.

It is also important to understand that a formal authority and power emerging from it, might not always be able to influence people in the desired manner as; in times of crisis and difficulties people view it as coercion. On the other hand leadership tends to create followers out of free will and choice without forcing them to accept anything thrown their way. Authority rarely provides a scope for feedback, constructive criticism or opinions of the people on whom it is exercised however leaders provide ample platform to their followers to voice their thoughts and feedback.

When dealing with adults, the sole use of authority to direct and discipline them hardly works, leadership provides a better approach of sharing and involving thus building rapports with followers and creating long term relationships. Authority can hardly make people change their attitudes and behaviors with lasting effects and results however a leader inspires followers through self modeled ways and hence leadership displays greater effectiveness in addressing attitudes and behaviors of people.

Exercising authority sometimes limits the approaches to arrive at solutions for issues and problems while leadership encourages people to look beyond the obvious and think innovatively and sometimes emerge with radical solutions.

Apart from it, the biggest difference between the two as cited by Stephen R Covey is the moral authority held by leaders over the followers which is absent in the case of power from authority. Within the organizational setup when leaders also have moral authority on their subordinates by establishing a synchrony in their words and actions; the rest of the structure and processes of the organization also get aligned to it, thus creating a robust and transparent culture.

Authoritative way of working also encourages individuals to work in silos while in the organizations of today; the leaders need to have a complete picture and coordinate with other functions and departments as and when required. It is indeed difficult for mangers and leaders to move out of their circle of authority and coordinate and interact with external people. However the need of the hour and the more effective approach to leadership and management is when leaders come out of their comfort zone and move from exercising authority on a small group to leading the entire organization.

Individuals, who do not rely on authority but lead people, are the ones who enjoy the privilege of their ideologies and thoughts practiced by later generations long after they are gone. Even with individuals who held positions of responsibilities, the ones who actually led their people are the ones remembered and followed.

- **Leadership and Motivation**

Motivation is a goal-oriented characteristic that helps a person achieve his objectives. It pushes an individual to work hard at achieving his or her goals. An executive must have the right leadership traits to influence motivation. However, there is no specific blueprint for motivation.

As a leader, one should keep an open perspective on human nature. Knowing different needs of subordinates will certainly make the decision-making process easier.

Both an employee as well as manager must possess leadership and motivational traits. An effective leader must have a thorough knowledge of motivational factors for others. He must understand the basic needs of employees, peers and his superiors. Leadership is used as a means of motivating others.

Given below are important guidelines that outline the basic view of motivation:

- Harmonize and match the subordinate needs with the organizational needs. As a leader, the executive must ensure that the business has the same morals and ethics that he seeks in his employees. He should make sure that his subordinates are encouraged and trained in a manner that meets the needs of the business.

- Appreciation and rewards are key motivators that influence a person to achieve a desired goal. Rewarding good/ exceptional behavior with a small token of appreciation, certificate or letter can be a great motivator. If a certificate is awarded to a person, it should mention the particular act or the quality for which the individual is being rewarded.

- Being a role model is also a key motivator that influences people in reaching their goals. A leader should set a good example to ensure his people to grow and achieve their goals effectively.

- Encouraging individuals to get involved in planning and important issues resolution procedure not only motivates them, but also teaches the intricacies of these key decision-making factors. Moreover, it will help everyone to get better understanding of their role in the organization. The communication will be unambiguous and will certainly attract acknowledgement and appreciation from the leader.

- Developing moral and team spirit certainly has a key impact on the well-being of an organization. The metal or emotional state of a person constitutes his or her moral fabric. A leader's actions and decisions affect the morale of his subordinates. Hence, he should always be aware of his decisions and activities. Team spirit is the soul of the organization. The leader should always make sure his subordinates enjoy performing their duties as a team and make themselves a part of the organization's plans.

- A leader should step into the shoes of the subordinates and view things from subordinate's angle. He should empathize with them during difficult times. Empathizing with their personal problems makes them stronger-mentally and emotionally.

- A meaningful and challenging job accomplished inculcates a sense of achievement among employees. The executive must make their employees feel they are performing an important work that is necessary for the organization's well-being and success. This motivational aspect drives them to fulfill goals.

Remember, **"To become an efficient leader, you must be self-motivated"**. You must know your identity, your needs and you must have a strong urge to do anything to achieve your goals. Once you are self-motivated, only then you can motivate others to achieve their goals and to harmonize their personal goals with the common goals of the organization.

- **Emotional Intelligence for Leaders**

An organization is made up of people and when people are involved, emotions automatically come into play, and a workplace is no different. It would be unwise to assume that a workplace is all objective, no-emotion only performance kind of a packed room where hormones have no scope to creep in however the fact is that emotions alone are the biggest motivator or de-motivator of an employee. The emotions alone, govern the performance and efficiency of a worker and had it not been the case, we would have never talked about the importance of work-life balance and for the present context, the need of emotionally intelligent leaders.

The current times are very dynamic not just economically but also socially where the social fabric is rapidly evolving due to globalization and other influences. The average age of the workforce is reducing and the leaders now look forward to managing people belonging to different cultures and backgrounds. In such a situation, it is important for a leader to be highly sensitized to the emotional aspects of his/her transactions with people. Emotional Intelligence is basically the ability to recognize and understand one's own feelings and emotions as well as those of others and use that information to manage emotions and relationships. The 4 important aspects of EI as proposed by Daniel Goleman are:

- Self Awareness
- Self Management
- Social Awareness
- Relationship Management or Social Skills

A leader tends to have a huge influence on the thoughts and motivation of people. He/she has the capacity to enthuse optimism and confidence in the followers and lead them to constructive endeavors which is called resonance and on the other hand they can negatively influence them to destruct, e.g of such leaders being Hitler and d Osama Bin Laden which is opposite to resonance called desonance.

Leaders are closely observed in terms of their body language, facial expressions etc. So, it is important for a leader to consider the non-verbal form of expressions as well, which may positively or negatively influence followers.

Therefore, if a leader is talking about ethics in business with a slightly unconvinced and bemused look on his face, the followers make a note of it and the message is not received by them. A leader has to act as a role model too, supporting his statements, ideologies and values with appropriate actions.

As a leader one also has to be aware of one's own capabilities and weaknesses, it is difficult to accept guidance from a leader who is not self aware. As managers, leaders have to empathize as well with the situations, emotions, aspirations and motivations of the subordinates. A decreasing performance of a team member might be because of a number of reasons, a disruptive worker might be facing motivation issues and a subordinate who uses abusive language with others might be lacking confidence in his own abilities. A leader needs to discern facts and try and reach to deeper levels and understand things beyond obvious.

Apart from the above reasons, Emotional Intelligence is also important because the followers or subordinate expect it from their leaders. A subordinate working closely with the manager would expect the manager to understand his situation and priorities. And not surprisingly, whether manger does so or not, affects his level of commitment and performance at work. A leader has to suitably know and understand when he/she needs to be directive and when he needs to delegate.

He/she needs to be aware, when the team members are acting as one unit and when there are differences.

It is sometimes awkward to address emotional aspects of transactions between people but leaders need to understand the importance and relevance of it as it has a huge impact on the performance outcomes. While conducting reviews and development dialogues, the feedback has to be delivered in a manner which is acceptable. The leader needs to be sensitive to the insecurities and apprehensions of the subordinates which sometimes might be expressed and sometimes kept undisclosed. At the senior level it is all the more important as the senior executives find it hard to clearly outline their anxieties and differences and the leader has to anticipate some of them.

So, to be able to attract and retain talented subordinates and keep them motivated, a leader needs to brush up on his people skills and emotional intelligence, as all of them are not born with the charisma to hold people. Fortunately, emotional intelligence with practice and carefully directed efforts can be increased.

- **Organizational Leadership**

Organizations need strong leadership for optimum effectiveness. Leadership, as we know, is a trait which is both inbuilt and can be acquired also. **Organizational leadership** deals with both human psychology as well as expert tactics. Organizational leadership emphasizes on developing leadership skills and abilities that are relevant across the organizations. It means the potential of the individuals to face the hard times in the industry and still grow during those times. It clearly identifies and distinguishes the leaders from the managers. The leader should have potential to control the group of individuals.

An ideal organizational leader should not dominate over others. He should guide the individuals under him, give them a sense of direction to achieve organizational goals successfully and should act responsibly. He should be optimistic for sure. He should be empathetic and should understand the need of the group members. An organizational leader should not only lead others individually but also manage the actions of the group.

Individuals who are highly ambitious, have high energy level, an urge to lead, self-confidence, intelligence, have thorough knowledge of job, are honest and flexible are more likely to succeed as organizational leaders. Individuals who learn the organizational leadership develop abilities and skills of teamwork, effective communication, conflict resolution, and group problem solving techniques. Organizational leaders clearly communicate organizational mission, vision and policies; build employees morale, ensure efficient business operations; help employees grow professionally and contribute positively towards organizations mission.

- **Tips for Effective Organizational Leadership**

1. A leader must lead himself, only then he can lead others. He must be committed on personal and professional front, and must be responsible. He must be a role model for others and set an example for them.

2. A leader must boost up the morale of the employees. He should motivate them well so that they are committed to the organization. He should be well acquainted with them, have concern for them and encourage them to take initiatives. This will result in more efficient and effective employees and ensure organizational success.

3. A leader must work as a team. He should always support his team and respect them. He should not hurt any employee. A true leader should not be too bossy and should not consider him as the supreme authority. He should realize that he is part of the organization as a whole.

Organizational leadership involves all the processes and possible results that lead to development and achievement of organizational goals. It includes employees' involvement, genuineness, effective listening and strategic communication.

- ## Leadership Ethics - Traits of an Ethical Leader

Ethics refer to the desirable and appropriate values and morals according to an individual or the society at large. Ethics deal with the purity of individuals and their intentions. Ethics serve as guidelines for analyzing "what is good or bad" in a specific scenario. Correlating ethics with leadership, we find that ethics is all about the leader's identity and the leader's role.

Ethical theories on leadership talk about two main things: (a) The actions and behaviour of leaders; and (b) the personality and character of leaders. It is essential to note that **"Ethics are an essential to leadership"**. A leader drives and influences the subordinates / followers to achieve a common goal, be it in case of team work, organizational quest, or any project. It is an ethical job of the leader to treat his subordinates with respect as each of them has unique personality. The ethical environment in an organization is built and developed by a leader as they have an influential role in the organization and due to the fact that leaders have an influence in developing the organizational values.

- **An effective and ethical leader has the following traits / characteristics:**

✓ **Dignity and respectfulness:** He respects others. An ethical leader should not use his followers as a medium to achieve his personal goals. He should respect their feelings, decision and values. Respecting the followers implies listening effectively to them, being compassionate to them, as well as being liberal in hearing opposing viewpoints. In short, it implies treating the followers in a manner that authenticate their values and beliefs.

✓ **Serving others:** He serves others. An ethical leader should place his follower's interests ahead of his interests. He should be humane. He must act in a manner that is always fruitful for his followers.

✓ **Justice:** He is fair and just. An ethical leader must treat all his followers equally. There should be no personal bias. Wherever some followers are treated differently, the ground for differential treatment should be fair, clear, and built on morality.

✓ **Community building:** He develops community. An ethical leader considers his own purpose as well as his followers' purpose, while making efforts to achieve the goals suitable to both of them. He is considerate to the community interests. He does not overlook the followers' intentions.

He works harder for the community goals.

✓ **Honesty:** He is loyal and honest. Honesty is essential to be an ethical and effective leader. Honest leaders can be always relied upon and depended upon. They always earn respect of their followers. An honest leader presents the fact and circumstances truly and completely, no matter how critical and harmful the fact may be. He does not misrepresent any fact.

It is essential to note that leadership is all about values, and it is impossible to be a leader if you lack the awareness and concern for your own personal values. Leadership has a moral and ethical aspect. These ethics define leadership. Leaders can use the above mentioned traits as yardsticks for influencing their own behaviour.

- **Leadership Strategy - Which Leadership Style to Follow ?**

Without an effective leadership strategy, it is believed, that the organizational strategies do not work. Best players in a team do not guarantee success without a great coach, similarly, work teams may not function effectively if leaders do not follow an appropriate leadership strategy.

To understand leadership styles here are three scenarios - *Scenario 1* - A Teacher gives a question to the class full of students, however, solves it for them; *Scenario 2* - A Teacher gives the question to the students and observes how students solve them; *Scenario 3* - A Teacher gives a question to the students and moves around the class, observes the students, and helps wherever required. Scenario 1 was "Leading from the Front", Scenario 2 was **"Supportive Leadership Style"**, and Scenario 3 was **"Interactive Leadership Style"**. Besides this the leadership styles / strategies could be based on personality traits like Directive Leadership, Structured Leadership, Intuitive Leadership, or Process Driven leadership.

Here are some tips while selecting leadership strategy / style:

✓ A leader must be aware of his / her personality traits and those of his team members / followers to understand which leadership style will be most effective.

✓ A leader may not adopt a consistent leadership all through his / her career. Situational Leadership helps addressing varied needs / expectations of the followers as he the leader adopts a strategy based on a situation he / she is in. In case a leader has a self-reliant team, he needs to be using a directive leadership style or lead form the front. He could instead delegate and provide inputs where necessary.

✓ A common mistake especially a lot of new leaders make is

to copy established / well know leaders. Remember, each situation is unique and so are the followers. A leadership style which may be suited to a well known leader may not be appropriate for your team. Make no mistake here - do not try and imitate other leaders.

✓ A leader will never be afraid of trying new approach to solve a work problem or address a conflicting situation. It is quite a possibility that a leader adopts a style that is not by the book.

✓ A leader must keep enhancing his / her leadership skills. While on the job experience matters a lot, getting enrolled into leadership courses after detailed evaluation of the program and feedback of the participants will help implementing a leadership style more effectively.

It is often said that good leaders are born and not made; however, good leaders are those who are aware of their personality traits and also of their followers. They know which leadership style is to be adopted in a particular situation. Once this is done, there is a little challenge left for a leader to become a "good / great" leader.

- **Leadership Styles - Important Leadership Styles**

All leaders do not possess same attitude or same perspective. As discussed earlier, few leaders adopt the carrot approach and a few adopt the stick approach. Thus, all of the leaders do not get the things done in the same manner. Their style varies. The leadership style varies with the kind of people the leader interacts and deals with. A perfect/standard leadership style is one which assists a leader in getting the best out of the people who follow him.

Some of the important leadership styles are as follows:

Autocratic leadership style: In this style of leadership, a leader has complete command and hold over their employees/team. The team cannot put forward their views even if they are best for the team's or organizational interests. They cannot criticize or question the leader's way of getting things done. The leader himself gets the things done. The advantage of this style is that it leads to speedy decision-making and greater productivity under leader's supervision. Drawbacks of this leadership style are that it leads to greater employee absenteeism and turnover. This leadership style works only when the leader is the best in performing or when the job is monotonous, unskilled and routine in nature or where the project is short-term and risky.

The Laissez Faire Leadership Style: Here, the leader totally trusts their employees/team to perform the job themselves. He just concentrates on the intellectual/rational aspect of his work and does not focus on the management aspect of his work. The team/employees are welcomed to share their views and provide suggestions which are best for organizational interests. This leadership style works only when the employees are skilled, loyal, experienced and intellectual.

Democrative/Participative leadership style: The leaders invite and encourage the team members to play an important role in decision-making process, though the ultimate decision-making power rests with the leader. The leader guides the employees on what to perform and how to perform, while the employees communicate to the leader their experience and the suggestions if any. The advantages of this leadership style are that it leads to satisfied, motivated and more skilled employees. It leads to an optimistic work environment and also encourages creativity. This leadership style has the only drawback that it is time-consuming.

Bureaucratic leadership: Here the leaders strictly adhere to the organizational rules and policies. Also, they make sure that the employees/team also strictly follows the rules and procedures. Promotions take place on the basis of employees' ability to adhere to organizational rules. This leadership style gradually develops over time. This leadership style is more suitable when safe work conditions and quality are required. But this leadership style discourages creativity and does not make employees self-contented.

- **How to Create a Personal Leadership Brand ?**

Every leader has a personal leadership brand which might be carefully cultivated or intuitively perceived by leaders themselves and their followers. A personal leadership brand is an exclusive and a specific approach of a leader to address challenges and manage his/her transactions with their subordinates or followers. The best part of having a leadership brand is that it allows the flexibility to the leaders to define their own leadership objectives and then position themselves appropriately as per the need and situation. For example Lee Iacocca promulgated a leadership brand which was resolute, determined, persuasive and ready to take risks which helped him turn around Chrysler similarly Gandhi's leadership brand was that of integrity, honesty, principles, strength of character and above all truth.

It is essential for a leader to practice his/her leadership brand in thoughts and actions. How can a leader build up a leadership brand if they do not have one already. A leadership brand helps distinguish leaders and also outlines their approach, values, beliefs etc.

1. The first step definitely is identifying and establishing the results one wants to achieve by the end of a specific time period with a focus on preserving the interests of key stakeholders.

2. The second step becomes those distinguishing features with which one wants to be known as a leader. For e.g. one might identify drive for result as one's core strength area and can create a leadership brand based on the same

3. The next step becomes defining your identity. One might chose two or three word phrases to define their approach to leadership like Innovating to Excel etc

4. The last step becomes coming up with a leadership statement which conjuncts what one wants to be known for and what one wants to achieve

It is also important for leaders to check their leadership brand with seniors, subordinates and other stake-holders to understand their expectations from the role; and if any disconnect is pointed out, it needs to be incorporated.

Apart from the above aspects, leaders need to role model themselves and redefine their perceptions and ambitions to encompass the entire institution, which they represent. A leader needs to put the interests of the organization and stakeholders before his/her personal ambition and goals and strive to create success which is sustainable and does not need their constant presence.

The leaders need to understand that a personal leadership brand cannot be created overnight but credibility is earned the hard way, through years of perseverance. Once a leadership brand is created its acceptance and stability is established only after results are achieved. So, if a leader identifies certain goals but fails to achieve them, there are no takers for that leadership brand, similarly if a leader displays behaviors contradictory to what is outlined by his brand values, then also the credibility and respect of the brand is lost.

- **Level 5 Leadership**

We have always associated leadership with a very visible and popular role which gives you recognition and a larger than life status as a leader however the level 5 leadership proposes quite opposing characteristics of a successful leader. Jim Collins and his research team were exploring the factors that made good companies great way back in the 1960s. It was then that they stumbled upon the Level 5 leaders who were invariably at the helm of affairs of all the companies which went on to become great in their respective fields. Who exactly is a Level 5 leader? Collins describes Level 5 leader as Humility + Will = Level 5. They are the nurturing leaders who do not want credit but want success to sustain over a longer period of time, long after they are gone.

Level 5 leaders are modest, shy and fearless and possess the capability to transform an organization from good to great without portraying themselves as wizards with magic wands. They prefer talking about the company and the contribution of other people but rarely about their role or achievements. Let us have a look at the hierarchical level of leadership identified:

THE LEVEL 5 HIERARCHY

LEVEL 5 LEVEL 5 EXECUTIVE
Builds enduring greatness
through a paradoxical combination
of personal humility plus professional will.

LEVEL 4 EFFECTIVE LEADER
Catalyzes commitment to and vigorous pursuit
of a clear and compelling vision; stimulates
the group to high performance standards.

LEVEL 3 COMPETENT MANAGER
Organizes people and resources toward the effective
and efficient pursuit of predetermined objectives.

LEVEL 2 CONTRIBUTING TEAM MEMBER
Contributes to the achievement of group
objectives; works effectively with others in a group setting.

LEVEL 1 HIGHLY CAPABLE INDIVIDUAL
Makes productive contributions through talent, knowledge,
skills, and good work habits.

The Level 5 leadership clearly reestablishes the facts about a simply living and high thinking with an emphasis on personal humility taught by the older generations. The financial breakthroughs achieved by level 5 leaders prove that these characteristics can achieve tangible results as well. The most important example in this context can be cited of great world leaders like M.K. Gandhi and Abraham Lincoln, who always put their vision ahead of their egos. They came across as shy and defenseless people in their mannerism and speech but were hardly so when it came to actions. The other example from the business leaders who fitted perfectly into this category was Darwin E Smith who was the CEO of the paper company Kimberly-Clark and turned it around to become the biggest consumer paper product company. He was a unique mix of personal humility and will; combined with risk taking ability which made him a role model for the business leaders of today.

There are certain actions performed by Level 5 leaders which separate them from the rest of the leaders and senior executives.

- The first step if their ability to identify and include right people with them towards achieving goals. Unlike the traditional method of building strategies and then looking for the right people to carry them out, they take a different route. It's about getting the right people on board and then deciding on the destination.
- They also do not shy away from facing and accepting brutal truths and realities of data, numbers and situations but at the same time they do not lose hope of a better future.

- They also strive towards aligning consistent efforts towards a goal, rather than giving one massive push they believe in small but firm pushes to bring in the momentum.

- They also exercise their judgment to understand an aspect, in depth and thoroughly, rather than burdening themselves with myriad information.

- They practice and encourage a disciplined approach towards their work life and as visionaries use carefully identified technologies to give their businesses strategic advantage.

With the new concept of Level 5 leadership we come back to an age old question, can Level 5 leadership be learnt, if yes then how. According to Collins it is farfetched to suitably see whether it can be learnt or not but he surely identifies two categories of people, one who have the Level 5 Leadership in them, dormant, latent or unexpressed and others who do not have it.

So leaders who cannot look beyond their personal role, fame, achievements etc can hardly become Level 5 leaders. Only when they can put the larger good ahead of them, they transcend to the next level. This transition is not general but can be brought by some tragic accident, near death experiences or a life changing incident, as came across by Collins in his research. It would be appropriate to mention the name of M.K. Gandhi to understand it better. For Gandhi who had lived a comfortable life with a law degree from England had no experience of being oppressed by the ruling class until he was thrown out of a train despite carrying a first class ticket. His transition began from there, which later made him actively participate in the Indian Freedom Struggle.

Level 5 leadership is difficult to find and leaders who display it are a cut above the rest.

- **Situational Leadership - Meaning and Concept**

Leaders are essentially people who know their goals and have the power to influence the thoughts and actions of others to garner their support and cooperation to achieve these goals. In-case of leaders these goals are rarely personal and generally to serve the larger good. Ever since man was a hunter gatherer and lived in closely knit groups, they had leaders who led the hunting expeditions and took greater risk than the rest of the group members. In turn they were bestowed with larger share of hunting, respect and a higher position in the group. With changing times, how leadership is perceived has also changed, but, it remains an important aspect of social fabric nevertheless.

The initial theories proposed that leaders are born and cannot be created, there are certain distinct characteristics possessed by few men which make them leaders. [Read <u>Great Man Theory</u> and the <u>Trait Theory</u>]. However, for the current discussion we would try and take a closer look at another interesting theory which was proposed called Situational Leadership Theory. This theory says that the same leadership style cannot be practiced in all situations, depending upon the circumstance and environmental context the leadership style also changes. The pioneers of this theory were Kenneth Blanchard and Paul Hersey.

The model encourages the leaders to analyze a particular situation in depth and then lead in the most appropriate manner, suitable for that situation. The three aspects that need could be considered in a situation are:

- Employees' competences
- Maturity of the employees
- Complexity of the task
- Leadership style

In the Situational Leadership model, the leadership style has been divided into 4 types:

- **S1: Telling -** Telling style is associated with leaders who minutely supervise their followers, constantly instructing them about why, how and when of the tasks that need to be performed.

- **S2: Selling** - Selling style is when a leader provide controlled direction and is a little more open and allows two way communication between him/herself and the followers thus ensuring that the followers buy in the process and work towards the desired goals.

- **S3: Participating** - This style is characterized when the leaders seeks opinion and participation of the followers to establish how a task should be performed. The leader in this case tries creating relationship with the followers

- **S4: Delegating** - In this case, the leader plays a role in decisions that are taken but passes on or delegates the responsibilities of carrying out tasks to his followers. The leader however monitors and reviews the process.

It is also represented by a diagram most often which is below:

The developmental level of follower is an important indication for a leader to decide the most appropriate leadership style for them:

- **D4 - High Competence, High Commitment** - The followers who are identified in this category are the ones who have high competence and high commitment towards tasks to be performed. It might happen so that they turn out better than their leaders in performing these tasks. (For e.g. cricketing legend Sachin Tendulkar playing in the Indian cricket team under the captainship of Mahendra Singh Dhoni)

- **D3 - High Competence, Variable Commitment -** This category consists of followers who have the competence to do the job but their commitment level is inconsistent. They also tend to lack the confidence to go out and perform task alone. (E.g. President Barack Obama)

- **D2 - Some Competence, Low Commitment -** In this case, the followers have a certain level of competence which might be sufficient to do the job but they are low on commitment towards the tasks. Despite of having relevant skills to perform the task they seek external help when faced with new situations. (A team member made the trainer for new joiners)

- **D1 - Low Competence, High Commitment -** This category of followers may not have the specific skill required but they display a high level of commitment towards the task they have to perform, with confidence and motivation, they figure out ways to complete the tasks. (E.g. Mohandas Karamchand Gandhi, a lawyer by profession who spearheaded the Indian Freedom Struggle)

The above information regarding the style of leadership and the type of followers sure has a correlation to each other which forms the basis of situational leadership. So, a situational leader would try to accommodate his leadership style as per the situation and the level of competence and commitment of his followers. This information is also an important aspect to consider when senior leaders act as coaches for their subordinates in the organizations.

❖ Impact of Situational Leadership on Performance and Motivation

Leaders are role models who influence the culture, values,thoughts and actions of the organization and its people. The leadership style practiced by managers greatly influences the performance and productivity at the work place. The situation leadership model encourages managers to flexibly use their leadership style based on the situation and thus achieve effective results. Both at the middle managerial level where leaders work closely with people and at higher managerial level where leaders are responsible to a number of people, their approach has an impact on the motivational levels of the organization.

A leader needs to constantly inform him/herself of the motivational needs of the employees, one of simple factors of success cited in the organizations is a motivated workforce. The 4 leadership style of Telling, Selling, Participating and Delegating proposed in the situational leadership model can be used as per the motivational need of the subordinate. For example, for a senior manager who has been recently recruited and who boasts an illustrious career graph would need more responsibilities and opportunities to prove himself i.e. Delegating to remain motivated. On the other hand a fresher joining the organization may look at more Telling and a little participative approach to keep him/her motivated. A leader has to carefully evaluate and then decide on the right approach for the subordinate.

Situational Leadership has all the more relevance when teams work together especially across functions or locations. In these cases the team members might be physically separated from the leaders and the work situations might rapidly change, in such cases, maintaining the involvement and motivation level of team members becomes important. To create a high performance team that works effectively, the style that the leader would have to choose may be unique for each team.

Apart from this, a leader has to provide a vision to the people; it is the visions which help them direct and redirect their efforts towards it. In the recent times where changes are rapid in the organizations, the leaders have to be fully sensitized to what style would work the best, sometimes they might have to use a combination of styles to address issues effectively. For e.g. for a new change that is being introduced, the initial approach has to be Selling, where people are educated about the change, the next step becomes Telling, where the people have to be instructed as to how the change would be carried out. When the change starts settling in and people adopt it, they style can become Participating, where the people get an opportunity to partner in the change and take it ahead. The last change would then become delegating when the change can now be carried on by the others. The ultimate aim of any leader is to smoothly arrive at a stage where he/she can easily delegate tasks without worrying about its completion or effectiveness.

The leadership style also has a bearing when leaders are to act as mentors and coaches for their subordinates. The learning style of the subordinates can be interpreted in the terms of Telling, Selling, Participating and Delegating. Some subordinates learn when they know exactly what is to be done, some learn when they know the importance of the task, some learn when they understand the how of what is to be done, and ultimately some learn when they are actually allowed to perform the task. When a leader acts as a coach he/she has to keep in mind what works best for the coachee and the fact that what works for one might not work for the other.

❖ Influence of Situational Leadership Styles on Subordinate Development

As we know that the situational leadership theory

proposes that a leader needs to change his/her leadership style as per the situation and environment. Leaders also need to consider the level of their followers; to decide on a particular leadership style. Let us now try to explore, whether the leadership style practiced by the leader influences the subordinates at all and if they do then how does it happen?

In the organizational context a manager is not just a superior for his team of subordinates but is also their leader. This implies that as a manager he/she has to make sure that the subordinates are working cohesively as a unit to achieve department or function goals, and if a problem arises the manager has to step up and take the responsibility as a leader.

How would a manager ensure that each member and the team collectively are working towards that common goal? Sometimes, the contribution from each member is not equal, some are working and some are not, which often leads to imbalances and negativities in the team and work environment.

It is the leadership style practiced by the manager which to quite an extent is responsible for such a situation to arise. Every team has people who have different level of competence and commitment towards the work they do, some are pro-active and others need to be pushed. In either case, the role of the manager as a leader becomes all the more important where he/she needs to be flexible with the kind of leadership style they can practice with each subordinate.

Let's try to understand the relationship between leadership styles and subordinate development in a little detail. Recall the four situational leadership styles identified by Hersey and Blanchard. They were:

- Telling
- Selling
- Participating
- Delegating

Now, have a look at the following diagram which depicts the development level of the followers based on their competence and commitment towards their work.

So, which leadership style would be appropriate with each of these levels? A manager as a leader has to partner in the developmental journey of his/her subordinate. For a subordinate who is at a level D1, where he has low competence but high motivation, the leadership style could be Participative where the leader involves the subordinate and further motivates him to build on his competence to increase his/her effectiveness at tasks.

For a subordinate, who stands at a level D2 where he has some competence but lacks or shows inconsistent commitment, the leader can resort to the Telling style. In this case, the subordinate cannot be relied upon to complete the task without instructions and guidance. For the subordinates who fall into the category of D3 or high competence but variable commitment, the leadership style could be Selling as the leader would have to create a buy in from these subordinates to secure their commitment towards the task. Since they have the necessary competence to do the task, instructions are not required but such subordinates wish to see the value of the work they are doing to get committed to it.

And lastly, if the subordinate fall into the category of D4 where they have both high commitment and high motivation, the leadership style best suited could be Delegating, where the leaders need to understand, acknowledge and appreciate the competence and commitment of the subordinates and entrust them with responsibilities.

Leaders have to be aware of their surroundings and sensitized to the abilities and motivations of their followers/subordinates in order to be able to take effective decisions.

Introduction to Leadership Development

Leadership development entails nurturing, encouraging, incubating, and mentoring prospective leaders. In many organizations, the HR department in conjunction with senior management identifies potential leaders or fast trackers who are capable and ensures that they are motivated and encouraged to give their best. This form of mentoring and coaching of future leaders happens through organizational commitment to their development that includes sending them to specialized training programs, making them attend targeted workshops, and taking them to resorts and getaways with the express purpose of ensuring that these prospective leaders get all the encouragement and strategies to groom them into senior level positions.

It needs to be remembered that leadership development is not only about the organizational need for grooming prospective leaders but also to do with the candidates themselves showing the inclination and the aptitude to be groomed as leaders.

The point here is that **leadership development is a two-way process that is symbiotic with both the organization and the candidate showing interest in mutual success**. Only when both sides are keen on helping each other grow can true organizational development take place. This is the case with organizations like Infosys, Sony, and IBM, Fidelity etc where potential leaders are identified early on in their careers and given the necessary backing for them to blossom as true leaders. It needs to be mentioned that leadership in the current turbulent business landscape is a combination of traits and vision and hence potential leaders ought to have that rare combination of business acumen and risk taking along with visionary ideas with integrity. Integrity has been mentioned along with the rest as the financial crisis of 2008 proved that business leaders without integrity are a burden to the organization. Hence, these traits should be spotted and then adequate environmental support given so that leaders are groomed appropriately.

Leadership development is as much about traits as it is with experience and this is where the role of the mentors appears. Existing senior management leaders can help potential leaders perform better and give them tips and insights into how the business world operates so that they have an idea about how they have to respond to tricky and thorny issues. The point about real world experience is that many potential leaders might have the necessary traits and ambition but lack the insights into what makes for a successful leader in the real world. This is where the experience of the senior leaders in organizations helps as they can provide valuable guidance to the potential leaders on how to address tricky real world problems.

Finally, **leadership development entails commitment, patience, and skill and unless the potential leaders are committed to stay with the organization for an extended period, there is no point in grooming them**. Though many organizations have moved away from making the employees sign bonds, they still groom only those employees who have been with them for a while and who, in their estimation, are going to stick with the company for a longer term.

Leadership: Intrinsic vs Extrinsic Motivation

The steps that organizations can take to ensure that leaders are groomed by identifying potential leaders and then fast tracking them. This article looks at one trait of potential leaders that goes a long way in determining the success or otherwise of the leaders. This trait is motivation, the will to succeed, and the desire to do well, which is an integral part of leadership development. **Motivation is necessary for leaders to reach the top and the types of motivation are intrinsic and extrinsic motivation.** Intrinsic motivation is the will to succeed by changing oneself from within and extrinsic motivation is the performance that is driven by external rewards. The point here is that individuals have to be motivated from within and then they have to be rewarded with external benefits and benefits to achieve the best results in organizations.

This is clear from the emphasis that HR managers and senior executives place on matching rewards with performance that is first driven from within. To explain further, leaders have to be motivated to perform by a strong urge to succeed from within and then the external rewards have to match their performance.

Employees who are only motivated by external rewards do not make great leaders and conversely, employees who are not rewarded for their performance stagnate and lose morale. Hence, the strategic fit between intrinsic motivation and extrinsic motivation has to be just right for organizations to get the best from their employees. This is the reason many organizations go the whole distance in aligning incentives with performance. Unless employees are motivated from within, incentives and rewards can only help that much and unless high performers are rewarded appropriately, intrinsic motivation withers away.

The recent global economic crisis brought to the fore the system of flawed incentives that was in place in the investment banks and Wall Street firms. The point here is that though the bankers were performing well, the rewards were too high and this made them take unnecessary risks and not heed to the "inner voice" that guides us all in our daily life and career. Since this internal director compels us to be ethical and normative, the absence of conscience among the bankers led to their taking unnecessary risks with their business practices. The underlying incentives that were disproportionate to their actual performance made them oblivious to risk and ethics. Hence, the balance of intrinsic and extrinsic motivation has to be just right for high performance that is also ethical and normative in nature.

Finally, all of us need a higher vision for ourselves to succeed and this is the extra something that drives us to greater heights. As many theorists have pointed out, once the need for wealth and status is achieved, the higher needs of self-actualization or the need to be driven by vision appears. Hence, the conclusion is that intrinsic motivation is the driver for success as leaders and the rewards have to match this but not exceed beyond a certain point.

Appointing Home Grown Leaders to the Top Posts versus Bringing in Leaders from Outside

One of the thorny issues facing senior management in many organizations is the debate over grooming leaders from within and then appointing them to the top posts versus brining in leaders from outside and then making them the CEO. The debate is not confined to a particular country and occupies the energies of corporate leaders worldwide. This is because many organizations prefer that they have people at the helm who have come up the ranks as opposed to having outsiders take to the top slot. The issue is contentious because **appointing outsiders to the top slot evokes antipathy from those who have been overlooked and hence can lead to**

unnecessary tensions and lack of cooperation.

The way out for many boards of corporations is to conduct a search process wherein they consider both the homegrown talent as well as outsiders and decide purely based on merit and nothing else.

However, this is easier said than done since **appointing homegrown talent has its advantages**. First, these leaders know the organizational intricacies like the back of their hand and hence can be expected to bring familiarity and a sense of purpose to managing the organization given their knowledge of the bureaucracy and contacts. The point here is that since homegrown talent already knows the ropes of the organizational ladders, they are able to translate this advantage into actionable results. Further, they also have allegiance to power centers within the organizations and hence, this gives them an edge over outsiders, as they are able to navigate the treacherous waters of the organizational politics. However, this can also turn into a disadvantage as they would be beholden to certain power centers and hence would biased towards them and this leads to exacerbation of existing divisions.

On the other hand, **bringing in outsiders makes sense when the organization is in crisis and needs a fresh perspective**. The CEO drawn from the wider corporate world can start afresh without any leftover baggage and can ensure that he or she brings a new set of lens with which the organization can determine its vision. This is the case that works best when corporates are floundering because of intra organizational rivalries and hence bringing in outsiders would be a good idea to rejuvenate the organization. However, this is also easier said than done since there is a possibility of all factions ganging up on the new CEO and denying him or her chance to rebuild the organization.

The best possible course would be to have leaders groomed before the person at the top retires and hence, ensure that these leaders step into the shoes of the retiring leader. However, as the case of the Infosys leadership transition (we shall discuss this in detail in a subsequent article) proves, grooming leaders from within can also spark a boardroom war. Ultimately, the solution to this tricky issue needs to be found by recourse to a mixture of firmness and astuteness and there are no easy answers to the question as to whether homegrown leaders make the best choice or outsiders are the preferred alternative.

Transformational Leadership and its Value in the Corporate World

Transformational leadership is one of the many kinds of leadership that is usually on display in the real world. The reason for focusing on this particular type of leadership in this article is to highlight the need for transformational leadership in these tough times when the ability to articulate a vision and motivate the employees along with putting the company before self is badly needed.

The point here is that unless corporate leaders display transformational leadership in these turbulent times, the organizations that they head would not be able to withstand the headwinds of turbulence and navigate the choppy seas of competition. Examples of transformational leaders include the late legendary Steve Jobs of Apple, Bill Gates of Microsoft, Jack Welch of GE, and NR Narayana Murthy of Infosys. Along with these figures, the names of Aditya Birla and Ratan Tata come to mind when listing the hall of fame for transformational leaders.

Transformational leadership goes beyond normal leadership and as the name implies, it results in a complete rejuvenation of the company and a transformation of its place in the corporate world. For instance, the late Steve Jobs succeeded in altering consumer perceptions of computing, mobile technology, and the way in which media is consumed in the digital age. Similarly, Bill Gates can be credited with pioneering the personal computing revolution that has benefited Billions of people around the world and has transformed the landscape of the business world. Further, NR

Narayana Murthy can be said to have incubated a whole industry with his stewardship of Infosys that resulted in the IT sector in India taking off in a big way and emerging as a force to reckon with in the world. Finally, Ratan Tata and Aditya Birla can be credited with transforming what were essentially family owned businesses into a new look professionally managed conglomerates that redefined the map of the corporate world in the county and abroad.

Moreover, these figures succeeded in not only driving their companies to greater heights but also ensured that they were trailblazing and path breaking in their endeavors. For instance, Ratan Tata introduced the concept of the one Lakh Car in India, which ensured that millions of middle class consumers could convert their dream of owning a car into reality. Apart from Ratan Tata, Capt. Gopinath of the erstwhile Deccan Airways fame transformed the concept of aviation in India by providing the common person with the wherewithal and the connectivity needed by introducing the concept of SimplyFly or bringing flying to the masses.

We shall be discussing each of these figures and the traits of transformational leadership in other articles as well. It would suffice here to state that what each of these leaders had in common was a vision and the ability to translate it into actionable results and actualize it in practice. The point to be noted is that many leaders have the vision but fail to translate into reality. While some leaders (who are truly extraordinary) like the Late Legendary Dhirubhai Ambani had a combination of vision, mission, ambition, and hard work, which proved that he remains a towering figure in the list of transformational leaders.

Leadership for the 21st Century

The previous articles discussed the importance of transformational leadership in the corporate world. This article looks at the traits and attributes needed in the 21st century business landscape. Though the article on transformative leadership touched upon several aspects of leadership in the contemporary times, this article expands on it by including the role of ethics and value based leadership for the 21st century.

If there is one lesson to be learnt from the ongoing global financial crisis, it is that the business leaders failed miserably to implement value based systems and instead, gave free rein to greed and the pursuit of monetary rewards at the expense of everything else. Indeed, as the behavior of the bankers and the financial elite proved in the aftermath of the crisis, they were more interested in furthering their goals rather than thinking about the welfare of the people.

The business landscape of the 21st century is extremely

competitive and this umbers connected world means that leaders have extraordinary demands placed upon them. However, this does not mean that they take shortcuts to success and sacrifice ethics and principles at the altar of profits.

Instead, what is needed in the current times is that leaders must not only be transformative but also practice value-based leadership that gives importance to ethics and humanitarian principles. As the various articles on corporate social responsibility discussed, we can navigate this century only if we cooperate along with compete and only if we share along with earn. Hence, the solution to the crisis facing humanity is clear: we are all in the same boat and hence we sink or swim together. This is the place where leaders can display their leadership skills and ensure that they lead by example and not rock the boat and instead, teach others to steer it to safety.

Further, **leaders in the 21st century have another vital function i.e. they have to be the ideal role models for the coming generation** and since anyone who has grown up over the last two decades would testify, they have been influenced by leaders from all occupations. For instance, it is common for people in their thirties now to admire and idolize business leaders like Steve Jobs, Bill Gates, Jack Welch, and NR Narayana Murthy. In the same way, the upcoming generation needs to have the current leaders of the business world as role models and hence a holistic approach that does not put profits before people all the time, that does not place undue emphasis on making money as the sole aim, and finally, the transformative power of business to solve social problems with the leaders taking the lead, are traits and attributes that are needed from the leaders of the 21st century.

In this context, it is worth mentioning that the present generation is very cynical and disinterested in the leaders of the present because of the lack of these motivating characteristics from the leaders. Indeed, this is something that is food for thought for the present day leaders and something that they should actualize in practice.

The Trans leader: Strategy, Leadership, and the Soul

One of the big ideas being bandied about in recent times is the interaction of strategy, leadership, and the soul of organizations which when they work in tandem can create exceptional leaders in the 21st century business landscape. This is the premise of the book by Sertl and Huberman who have theorized that for leaders to be successful in the 21st century, they need a blend of strategy that is rethought every now and then, leadership that is dependent on sensing relevance in all areas of life and business, and finally, the integration of the values and inner beliefs of the individual with that of the organization. The point here is that for leaders to succeed in the 21st century landscape, an integrated model of leadership is what is needed and which Sertl and Huberman propose.

To take the first aspect, **strategy in this model of leadership is ever changing to reflect the fluid marketplace** where a rapid turnover of ideas, fads, and trends means that strategy has to be continuously refined and rethought.

Strategy in this case is not merely something that is drawn up every few years and then followed irrespective of the changes in the external world. Instead, strategy changes with each relevant change of the trends. Note the emphasis on the term relevant as strategy cannot change with each passing fad or trend and instead, the leader must evaluate the relevance of the trend to his or her business and then strategize accordingly. Moreover, there needs to be a dynamic strategy in place to tackle any tectonic shifts in the business world and hence strategy must not be static.

Next, **leadership ought to be responsive to complexity, ambiguity, and uncertainty**. There is no point for a leader to be smug in the confidence that he or she knows every detail of the business and hence does not see the need for working through these aspects. Further, the days of leadership based on knowledge and experience is outdated, as the "transleader" needs to be transformational in the sense that he or she should combine knowledge and experience along with an intuitive understanding of the three aspects listed above. The point here is that the Transleader must be able to intuit and sense the changes in the external world and react and respond accordingly.

The third aspect, which is revolutionary, is that **the Trans leader must be someone whose inner values and beliefs mirror that of the organization and vice versa**. Only through this integration would the organization's power and efficiency would be leveraged and the leader and the employees can find success and fulfillment in their careers. The point here is that the alignment of this "soul" across the customers, employees, and business partners is a fundamental necessity for the success of the leader and the organization. In conclusion, the organizations of the future would have trans leaders who can play a transformative role and by reenergizing the soul of the organizations, they can lead them to greater successes.

Three Traits of Effective Leadership

We have introduced the concept of Trans leader in the previous articles. We discussed how a leader who is integral to the organization and vice versa could prove to be an effective leader. Taking the discussion forward, this article reviews the three traits that make for effective leadership and separates leaders from followers. The three traits that are discussed here are character, vision, and relationship effectiveness. It needs to be mentioned that these three are not the only traits but more like these traits are essential to leadership. In other words, these traits are necessary but not exhaustive.

To take the first trait, **character of the leaders is important as it defines who they are, what they will do, and what they would not do, and what they stand for**. In other words, the individuals who have their values and beliefs in deep-rooted ways would be able to withstand the pressures and tests of their values and principles. Since leadership is all about being the final decision maker, it is important for the leaders to be committed to principle and be driven by values instead of merely pursuing the bottom line. Hence, the first trait of effective leadership is the strength of character that leaders have.

The next trait of effective leadership is the ability to be a visionary and have a sense of future possibilities. The point here is that leaders are individuals whom the followers look up to guide them towards the future and hence leaders ought to have visionary capabilities to actualize this need. We have examples from business, government, and society where true leaders like the late legendary Steve Jobs, Bill Gates, and Larry Paige and Sergei Brian of Google proved that they had game changing ideas about the future. The essence of 21st century leadership is not only about peering into the future but also making the future a place for the organization to thrive and succeed. In other words, leaders are those individuals who are not threatened by the future and instead like the legendary mythological prophets in every religion can show pathways to the future which the followers can follow.

The third trait is how effective the leaders are in personal relationships. Since most leaders realize that, the whole game of life is all about people and the relationships that one builds with those whom one encounters; effectiveness in personal relationships distinguishes the true leaders from the rest. Though this does not mean that leaders need only charisma or be a people's person, the point here is that by nurturing and incubating relationships, the leaders can prove that their behavior towards others and the effectiveness, which they display in their relationships, pervades the whole organization and infects others positively to do the same.

Finally, it needs to be noted that leaders must find the organizations that they are comfortable in and hence their characteristics and the organizational DNA must be aligned to create a winning combination. After all, one can be the right person for the wrong job and the wrong person for the right job and what matters is whether one is the right person for the right job.

Reinventing Management for the 21st Century

A Failure of Leadership in Management ?

The world is facing unprecedented upheaval and chaos in virtually every sphere of human activity. Where it is economic crisis, climate change, resource depletion, failure of political systems, or the breakdown of the social order, there is only gloom and doom all over us. Hence, **the broader question is whether we have had a failure of leadership in the sense that there are no leaders in business or society who are able to show the way and lead us from the front**.

The narrower question is why did management thought that was responsible for so many achievements and improvements in material prosperity over the last century or so fail us so miserably. It is these questions that this article and subsequent articles explore to illuminate how a new generation of leaders in business and society emerge and provide us with exemplary leadership that would be known for decades.

Some Trends and how they are going to shape the future

First, the Millennial Generation or those born in the period 1980-1995 have come of age at a time when the world is in crisis. As discussed above, the problems are many but the options are limited. With social, economic, and political transformation, the present generation can again rejuvenate the world of business and chart a new course for humanity. Since this generation came of age when the internet was making its presence felt and are now experiencing the mobile wave, it is safe to say that the emerging generation would have the necessary knowledge and experience in the technologies of the future to make a difference to the world of business. The other trend is that though people are living and working longer, they no longer are loyal to a single organization and instead, are only loyal to their professional identities. For instance, while the norm in the earlier generations was to stick to a job throughout ones working life, now it is considered something of an aberration if people do not change jobs.

Need to Reinvent Leadership and Management

These trends discussed above have led to a fundamental change in the economic logic of the firm. If the earlier management thought was about capital as the scarce resource and the strategic imperative of the firm was to transform inputs into outputs in an efficient manner, now knowledge is the scarce resource and firms succeed not only because of the efficiencies of their processes but also because of creativity and innovation. Hence, these aspects have led to a basic change in the way management and leadership is understood and therefore, there is a compelling case to be made to reinvent management.

Closing Thoughts

Finally, we discussed the positive aspects (reinventing leadership) and the negative aspects (the gloomy situation, as it exists now). For all future leaders, there is a message here: which aspect you chose to be the basis of your worldview would depend on your attitude and your approach to life. If you think that the future is all gloomy, then no amount of persuasion is going to make you change your mind. On the other hand, if you think that the future holds promise, then you can start thinking seriously, about how you can revitalize the field of business and management. The choice is yours.

Six Essential Social Media Skills that Every Leader Should Have

The social media revolution has taken the business world by storm. Few areas of business and society have been left untouched by the social media revolution. Concomitant with this trend, companies and business leaders have realized the immense power of social media and have started to tune their strategies accordingly. **This article discusses six essential social media skills that every leader must have to succeed in the world of Web 2.0**

1. Becoming a Producer

Business leaders must incorporate social media in their communications by producing and sharing rich media in their blogs and by opening Facebook and Twitter accounts through which they can communicate to their stakeholders. Of course, this is easier said than done as most business leaders are behind the curve where social media is concerned. To alleviate this shortcoming, business leaders have to learn to use technology more effectively and more efficiently. This means that they would have to upgrade their technical skills and become social media savvy. This literacy and expertise in using social media would be a major advantage to them as they go about communicating to their stakeholders.

2. Becoming a Distributor

The convergence of vertical broadcast media and horizontal participatory media means that the business leaders must master the knowledge of this interplay between these very different paradigms at work. For instance, traditional communication is largely hierarchical and follows command and control flow. On the other hand, social media follows system dynamics that determine whether the content goes viral or not and hence, business leaders must become experts in controlling the distribution of content that would let them influence the flow of communication throughout the organization. Knowing what to say and how to say are as important as the distribution of these messages to the wider audience.

3. Becoming a Recipient

A common refrain one hears in the information age is that we are besieged with information overload. Drowning in a never reducing flood of Facebook posts, tweets, and emails, business leaders can get lost in this electronic maze that would impair their ability to sift through the content and determine what is useful or not. Given the fact that traditionally business leaders have had assistants to wade through the information and give them what is necessary, they might have to employ web savvy staff to do this for them in the changing world of web 2.0

4. Becoming an Advisor and Orchestrator

Once the business leaders realize the importance of web 2.0 for their organizations, the next task is to ensure that they let this insight percolate throughout the organization. In other words, they have to become change agents wherein they would harvest the potential of social media by inspiring their employees to embrace social media effectively and efficiently. To do this, they must have the skills described in the three sections above and on top of that, they must don the hat of evangelicals who trumpet the advantages of social media to their employees.

5. Becoming an Architect

The social media revolution has challenged the traditional conceptions of organizational communication, as there is a thin line between free exchange of information throughout the organization and the risk of irresponsible use that poses existential threats to the organizations. For instance, it is common in many firms to ban the use of social media by the employee during the time they spend in office. Instead of these autarkic responses, business leaders must develop appropriate strategies that would merge vertical accountability with horizontal collaboration. In other words, the merger of organizational hierarchical communication with that of informal networks of communication is the challenge before business leaders.

6. Becoming an Analyst

Finally, business leaders must not only leverage social media for their organizational success but also be ahead of the curve by riding the wave of change and anticipating the next paradigm shift. As the next generation internet of things is already on the horizon, business leaders must use all their intellect and experience to see how their organizations can profit from the coming changes. This means wearing multiple hats at once and ensuring that they are ahead of the curve instead of behind it.

Social Stratification and Hierarchy: What Business Leaders Ought to Know

Rise above Social Stratification

All societies are stratified and have elements of hierarchy amongst their members. If the notion of Varna or Caste is prevalent in the East, then the notion of class and race is prevalent in the west. In recent decades, with the advent of modernity and postmodernism, there has been a tendency among social scientists to dismiss the concept of stratification and insist that societies become egalitarian. Without getting into the merits and demerits of particular types of social stratification, it is important to remember that in all societies, the coalescing of people around specific identities forms the glue that binds them together and in turn gives coherence and sense of purpose to society. Of course, this is not to say that without racial or ethnic identities, societies would flounder. Indeed, with modern notions, the concept of these groupings has become antiquated. The point that is being made here is that in the absence of formalized structures and institutions that promote equality, the ethnic and the racial groupings provide their members with a sense of security and a fallback option in hard times. Indeed, the success of the East in recent times has been attributed to the prevalence of family values, group identity, and the networks of racial and ethnic groups that provide the much-needed support for starting new ventures or growth of existing ones. On the other hand, the widening income inequality in the West, which is another form of stratification, has been blamed for the deterioration and degeneration in those countries.

Hierarchy and its uses and disadvantages

Turning to the concept of hierarchy, it is indeed the case that any organization or grouping of people has to be hierarchical if decision-making and responsibility as well as accountability of these groupings is to actualize. In other words, though most of us hate the fact that hierarchy among peoples make some superior and others inferior, for purposes of cohesion and coherence as well as discipline and order, some semblance of control should be present which is provided by hierarchy. As mentioned earlier, this is not a justification for the prevalence of group identities based on narrow conceptions of human nature. Rather, the examination of what are trends in societies is the focus of this article and as empirical research shows, these groupings are very much present both in the West (based on income and class along with race) as well as in the East (based on ethnic, religious, and other social groupings). Hence, any policymaker or business leader has to necessarily take into account these realities and without paying too much importance to the divisions, has to work with them and within them as well as rise above them if he or she has to make an impact on the organizations that they head.

Be Global in Attitude yet Local in Execution

The concepts of stratification and hierarchy are closely intertwined, as one cannot exist without the other. Though this is reprehensible fact that some groups are deemed superior to others, the fact that business leaders ought to understand the different social structures and base their strategies on shrewd observation cannot be denied. As has been emphasized throughout this article, the best approach would be one where hierarchy is determined based on merit and stratification is absent except where the need for decision-making and execution of strategy is concerned. in other words, the truly great business leaders are aware of the societal differences but rise above them and ensure that their strategies are realistic without getting caught in the inter group and intra group warfare and strife.

Closing Thoughts

Finally, it is high time we acknowledge the fact that the 21st century belongs to global leaders who realize the importance of cosmopolitan leadership rather than antiquated divisions. On the other hand, they need to be cognizant of the local realities which would make them avoid the mistake of forcing global notions on the society without a clear understanding of the on the ground situation.

Leadership in the Face of Adversity

The best leaders are those who can face adversity and turnaround their companies from times of trouble to positions of strength. Throughout history, the leaders who were feted and achieved fame are those who took charge during times of crisis and managed to actualize victory. Similarly, in recent decades, the business world has seen a surfeit of leaders who stepped in when their companies were going through a rough patch and with their leadership ensured that they could revive and rejuvenate their companies. For instance, the legendary Lee Iacocca who was at the helm in Ford Motors took over the leadership of another auto major, Chrysler when the company was going through troubled times and in a matter of a few years ensured that it turned the corner. The case of the late Steve Jobs is another example of how he was recalled to Apple when the company was facing adversity and shrinking market share and with his game changing approach to business ensured that Apple is the most profitable company in the world. In recent weeks, the respected founder of Infosys, NR Narayana Murthy, has been recalled from retirement and tasked with the job of restoring the company to its previous dominant position.

The Elements of Leadership in Adversity

What these examples tell us is that true leadership is a phenomenon that thrives on challenges and the authentic leaders are those who can turn adversity into opportunity. These leaders follow the maxim that when the going gets tough, the tough get going. More often than not, they lead by example and from the front, which means that they set a benchmark for the employees to follow which often motivates the employees to perform better and actualize their potential. In many cases, leadership in times of adversity works by rejuvenating the company through stirring words and actions and the latter are more important as the nuts and bolts of leadership lies in execution. The example of how Ratan Tata turned the TATA group around is a case in point as to how leaders need to work more and talk less and ensure that execution is as important as or more important than planning and conceptualization. When one considers businesses that are moribund or near to failure, we find that bringing in leaders who can inspire and actualize success helps a lot in reviving the fortunes of these companies. For instance, the example of how the public sector enterprises in India have been made profitable and that too worthy of high market capitalization from a situation where they were close to being shut tells us that collective leadership in the face of adversity is as important as charismatic and visionary leadership.

The Characteristics of Leadership in Adversity

The key point to be noted here is that anyone can ride the success of companies but it takes a real leader with vision, mission, and hard work to turn around companies that are struggling. One of the important aspects of such leadership is that they must have a team of peers and managers who are as committed to the revival of the company as the leader. This is critical and necessary for leaders tor turnaround the companies. Another aspect about such leadership is that they must be given time to succeed as transformations do not happen overnight unless one expects miracles, which is something most business leaders discount. Therefore, time, patience, effort, and cooperation are all factors that play a crucial role in determining whether the leader succeeds in his or her mission. The case of the former Defense Secretaries, Robert McNamara in the 1960s, and Robert Gates in recent years illustrates that for deep changes to actualize; the leaders need time, patience, and energy as well as a single-minded devotion to their tasks.

Leadership Theories - Important Theories of Leadership

Just as management knowledge is supported by various theories, the leadership function of management too is authenticated by various theories. While the behavioural theories of leadership focused on discovering the constant relationship between leadership behaviours and the group performance, the contemporary theories emphasized the significance of situational factors (such as stress level, job structure, leader's intelligence, followers' traits, etc.) as well.

Some of the **important leadership theories** are as follows:

- Blake and Mouton's Managerial Grid
- House's Path Goal Theory
- Great Man Theory
- Trait Theory
- Leadership-Member Exchange (LMX) Theory
- Transformational Leadership
- Transactional Leadership
- Continuum of Leadership Behaviour
- Likert's Management System
- Hersey Blanchard Model
- Fiedler's Contingency Model

Transformational Leadership Theory

Creating high-performance workforce has become increasingly important and to do so business leaders must be able to inspire organizational members to go beyond their task requirements. As a result, new concepts of leadership have emerged - transformational leadership being one of them.

Transformational leadership may be found at all levels of the organization: teams, departments, divisions, and organization as a whole. Such leaders are visionary, inspiring, daring, risk-takers, and thoughtful thinkers. They have a charismatic appeal. But charisma alone is insufficient for changing the way an organization operates. For bringing major changes, transformational leaders must exhibit the following four factors:

Figure 1: Model of Transformational Leadership

✓ **Inspirational Motivation:** The foundation of transformational leadership is the promotion of consistent vision, mission, and a set of values to the members. Their vision is so compelling that they know what they want from every interaction. Transformational leaders guide followers by providing them with a sense of meaning and challenge. They work enthusiastically and optimistically to foster the spirit of teamwork and commitment.

- ✓ **Intellectual Stimulation:** Such leaders encourage their followers to be innovative and creative. They encourage new ideas from their followers and never criticize them publicly for the mistakes committed by them. The leaders focus on the "what" in problems and do not focus on the blaming part of it. They have no hesitation in discarding an old practice set by them if it is found ineffective.

- ✓ **Idealized Influence:** They believe in the philosophy that a leader can influence followers only when he practices what he preaches. The leaders act as role models that followers seek to emulate. Such leaders always win the trust and respect of their followers through their action. They typically place their followers needs over their own, sacrifice their personal gains for them, ad demonstrate high standards of ethical conduct. The use of power by such leaders is aimed at influencing them to strive for the common goals of the organization.

- ✓ **Individualized Consideration:** Leaders act as mentors to their followers and reward them for creativity and innovation. The followers are treated differently according to their talents and knowledge. They are empowered to make decisions and are always provided with the needed support to implement their decisions.

The common examples of transformational leaders are Mahatma Gandhi and Obama.

Criticisms of Transformational Leadership Theory

- Transformational leadership makes use of impression management and therefore lends itself to amoral self promotion by leaders
- The theory is very difficult to e trained or taught because it is a combination of many leadership theories.
- Followers might be manipulated by leaders and there are chances that they lose more than they gain.

Implications of Transformational Leadership Theory

The current environment characterized by uncertainty, global turbulence, and organizational instability calls for transformational leadership to prevail at all levels of the organization. The followers of such leaders demonstrate high levels of job satisfaction and organizational commitment, and engage in organizational citizenship behaviors. With such a devoted workforce, it will definitely be useful to consider making efforts towards developing ways of transforming organization through leadership.

Transactional Leadership Theory

The transactional style of leadership was first described

by Max Weber in 1947 and then by Bernard Bass in 1981. This style is most often used by the managers. It focuses on the basic management process of controlling, organizing, and short-term planning. The famous examples of leaders who have used transactional technique include McCarthy and de Gaulle.

Transactional leadership involves motivating and directing followers primarily through appealing to their own self-interest. The power of transactional leaders comes from their formal authority and responsibility in the organization. The main goal of the follower is to obey the instructions of the leader. The style can also be mentioned as a 'telling style'.

The leader believes in motivating through a system of rewards and punishment. If a subordinate does what is desired, a reward will follow, and if he does not go as per the wishes of the leader, a punishment will follow. Here, the exchange between leader and follower takes place to achieve routine performance goals.

These exchanges involve four dimensions:

✓ **Contingent Rewards:** Transactional leaders link the goal to rewards, clarify expectations, provide necessary resources, set mutually agreed upon goals, and provide various kinds of rewards for successful performance. They set SMART (specific, measurable, attainable, realistic, and timely) goals for their subordinates.

✓ **Active Management by Exception:** Transactional leaders actively monitor the work of their subordinates, watch for deviations from rules and standards and taking corrective action to prevent mistakes.

✓ **Passive Management by Exception:** Transactional leaders intervene only when standards are not met or when the performance is not as per the expectations. They may even use punishment as a response to unacceptable performance.

✓ **Laissez-faire:** The leader provides an environment where the subordinates get many opportunities to make decisions. The leader himself abdicates responsibilities and avoids making decisions and therefore the group often lacks direction.

Assumptions of Transactional Theory

- Employees are motivated by reward and punishment.
- The subordinates have to obey the orders of the superior.
- The subordinates are not self-motivated. They have to be closely monitored and controlled to get the work done from them.

Implications of Transactional Theory

The transactional leaders overemphasize detailed and short-term goals, and standard rules and procedures. They do not make an effort to enhance followers' creativity and generation of new ideas. This kind of a leadership style may work well where the organizational problems are simple and clearly defined. Such leaders tend to not reward or ignore ideas that do not fit with existing plans and goals.

The transactional leaders are found to be quite effective in guiding efficiency decisions which are aimed at cutting costs and improving productivity. The transactional leaders tend to be highly directive and action oriented and their relationship with the followers tends to be transitory and not based on emotional bonds.

The theory assumes that subordinates can be motivated by simple rewards. The only 'transaction' between the leader and the followers is the money which the followers receive for their compliance and effort.

Difference between Transactional and Transformational Leaders

Transactional leadership	Transformational Leadership
Leadership is responsive	Leadership is proactive
Works within the organizational culture	Work to change the organizational culture by implementing new ideas
Transactional leaders	Transformational leaders motivate

make employees achieve organizational objectives through rewards and punishment	and empower employees to achieve company's objectives by appealing to higher ideals and moral values
Motivates followers by appealing to their own self-interest	Motivates followers by encouraging them to transcend their own interests for those of the group or unit

Conclusion

The transactional style of leadership is viewed as insufficient, but not bad, in developing the maximum leadership potential. It forms as the basis for more mature interactions but care should be taken by leaders not to practice it exclusively, otherwise it will lead to the creation of an environment permeated by position, power, perks, and politics.

Continuum of Leadership Behaviour

The leadership continuum was originally written in 1958 by Tannenbaum and Schmidt and was later updated in the year 1973. Their work suggests a continuum of possible leadership behavior available to a manager and along which many leadership styles may be placed. The continuum presents a range of action related to the degree of authority used by the manager and to the area of freedom available to non-managers in arriving at decisions. A broad range of leadership styles have been depicted on the continuum between two extremes of autocratic and free rein (See figure 1). The left side shows a style where control is maintained by a manager and the right side shows the release of control. However, neither extreme is absolute and authority and freedom are never without their limitations.

The Tannenbaum and Schmidt continuum can be related to McGregor's supposition of Theory X and Theory Y. Boss-centered leadership is towards theory X and subordinate-centered leadership is towards theory Y.

Figure 1: Continuum Leadership Behavior.

Autocratic → Free-rein
(Boss-centered Leadership) (Subordinate-centered Leadership)

Use of authority by manager

Area of freedom for subordinates

Manager makes decisions and announces

Manager sells decisions

Manager presents ideas and invites suggestions

Manager presents tentative decision subject to change

Manager presents problems, gets suggestions and makes decisions

Manager defines limits, asks group to make decision

Manager permits subordinates to function within limits defined by superior

A manager is characterized according to degree of control that is maintained by him. According to this approach, four main styles of leadership have been identified:

- **Tells:** The manager identifies a problem, chooses a decision, and announces this to subordinates. The subordinates are not a party to the decision making process and the manager expects them to implement his decisions as soon as possible.

- **Sells:** The decision is chosen by the manager only but he understands that there will be some amount of resistance from those faced with the decision and therefore makes efforts to persuade them to accept it.

- **Consults:** Though the problem is identified by the manager, he does not take a final decision. The problem is presented to the subordinates and the solutions are suggested by the subordinates.

- **Joins:** The manager defines the limits within which the decision can be taken by the subordinates and then makes the final decision along with the subordinates.

According to Tannenbaum and Schmidt, if one has to make a choice of the leadership style which is practicable and desirable, then his answer will depend upon the following three factors:

- *Forces in the Manager:* The behavior of the leader is influenced by his personality, background, knowledge, and experience. These forces include:
  i. Value systems
  ii. Confidence in subordinates
  iii. Leadership inclinations
  iv. Feelings of security in an uncertain situation
- *Forces in the subordinate:* The personality of the subordinates and their expectations from the leader influences their behavior. The factors include:
  i. Readiness to assume responsibility in decision-making
  ii. Degree of tolerance for ambiguity
  iii. Interest in the problem and feelings as to its importance
  iv. Strength of the needs for independence
  v. Knowledge and experience to deal with the problem
  vi. Understanding and identification with the goals of the organization

If these factors are on a positive side, then more freedom can be allowed to the subordinate by the leader.

- *Forces in the situation:* The environmental and general situations also affect the leader's behavior. These include factors like:
  i. Type of organization

ii.   Group effectiveness

iii.   Nature of the problem

iv.   Time pressure

When the authors updated their work in1973, they suggested a new continuum of patterns of leadership behavior. In this, the total area of freedom shared between managers and non-managers is redefined constantly by interactions between them and the environmental forces. This pattern was, however, more complex in comparison to the previous one.

Conclusion

According to Tannenbaum and Schmidt, successful leaders know which behavior is the most appropriate at a particular time. They shape their behavior after a careful analysis of self, their subordinates, organization, and environmental factors.

Likert's Management System

Rensis Likert and his associates studied the patterns and styles of managers for three decades at the University of Michigan, USA, and identified a four-fold model of management systems. The model was developed on the basis of a questionnaire administered to managers in over 200 organizations and research into the performance characteristics of different types of organizations. The four systems of management system or the four leadership styles identified by Likert are:

- **System 1 - Exploitative Authoritative:** Responsibility lies in the hands of the people at the upper echelons of the hierarchy. The superior has no trust and confidence in subordinates. The decisions are imposed on subordinates and they do not feel free at all to discuss things about the job with their superior. The teamwork or communication is very little and the motivation is based on threats.

- **System 2 - Benevolent Authoritative:** The responsibility lies at the managerial levels but not at the lower levels of the organizational hierarchy. The superior has condescending confidence and trust in subordinates (master-servant relationship). Here again, the subordinates do not feel free to discuss things about the job with their superior. The teamwork or communication is very little and motivation is based on a system of rewards.

- **System 3 - Consultative:** Responsibility is spread widely through the organizational hierarchy. The superior has substantial but not complete confidence in subordinates. Some amount of discussion about job related things takes place between the superior and subordinates. There is a fair amount of teamwork, and communication takes place vertically and horizontally. The motivation is based on rewards and involvement in the job.

- **System 4 - Participative:** Responsibility for achieving the organizational goals is widespread throughout the organizational hierarchy. There is a high level of confidence that the superior has in his subordinates. There is a high level of teamwork, communication, and participation.

The nature of these four management systems has been described by Likert through a profile of organizational characteristics. In this profile, the four management systems have been compared with one another on the basis of certain organizational variables which are:

- Leadership processes
- Motivational forces
- Communication process
- Interaction-influence process
- Decision-making process
- Goal-setting or ordering
- Control processes

On the basis of this profile, Likert administered a questionnaire to several employees belonging to different organizations and from different managerial positions (both line and staff). His studies confirmed that the departments or units employing management practices within Systems 1 and 2 were the lease productive, and the departments or units employing management practices within Systems 3 and 4 were the most productive.

Advantages

With the help of the profile developed by Likert, it became possible to quantify the results of the work done in the field of group dynamics. Likert theory also facilitated the measurement of the "soft" areas of management, such as trust and communication.

Conclusion

According to Rensis Likert, the nearer the behavioral characteristics of an organization approach System 4 (Participative), the more likely this will lead to long-term improvementin staff turnover and high productivity, low scrap, low costs, and high earnings.if an organization wants to achieve optimum effectiveness, then the ideal system

Leadership and Trust

Trust seems to be the key trait linked with leadership. A leader cannot lead if his followers do not trust him. A leader discovers the employees'/followers problems and tries to solve them, but it is the trust that his followers hold on him which tells whether the leaders retrieve the knowledge and intellectuality required to solve the problems. Trust can be defined as an optimistic belief that others will not perform (via words, acts, or final conclusions) in an opportunistic manner.

For trust to nurture, an appropriate atmosphere is needed. This responsibility rests with the leader in an organization. The employees will show absolute trust in the leaders when they observe ideal/excellent character in them. **Leaders play a crucial role in developing and maintaining trust of organizational employees**. Reliability, empathy and realization of individual/personal goals assist the leaders to gain trust of the employees/followers. When the employees show trust in a leader, they are ready to be exposed to the actions of the leader- self-assured that their interests and rights will not be harmed.

The primary facets of trust are:

- **Truth/Honesty**
- **Proficiency/Competency**
- **Commitment**
- **Reliability**
- **Sincerity/Openness**

A leader should keep his followers informed, be fair and objective, share his feelings, be honest, allow the followers to constantly direct their decisions, maintain their promises, and earn respect of the followers. All this will contribute in building trust upon the leaders.

A trust-centred leadership will offset worries, apprehensions, and low-morale by developing a trustworthy environment where employees feel secure, confident and keyed up. The employees will be ready to take initiative, give suggestions, share their views, feel unhesitant to take risk and will contribute completely in such an atmosphere of trust.

Due to instability and unpredictability of organizations today, building of trust between managers as leaders and their employees is essentially required.

How to be a Good Leader - What makes Leadership Effective ?

Leadership is a significant aspect of management. In order to ensure organizational success, co-operation from subordinates as well as greater efficiency, it is important for a manager to be a great, effective and a true leader. An effective and true leader is one who does not put himself before others. He is very humble, deferential and altruistic.

The required aspects of effective leadership are as follows:

- Motivation
- Commitment
- Self-sacrifice
- Honesty
- Determination
- Resourcefulness
- Daring
- Knowledge
- Good communication skills
- Passion
- Responsibility
- Judgement

Leadership is boosting an individual's performance to a greater benchmark, the developing of an individual's personality crossing its standard boundaries. It is a combo of mindframes, traits, skills, and knowledge. Leadership means adhering to the following principles:

- Respect your followers.
- Acknowledge the followers efforts if there is success, and do not blame them for any failure.
- Encourage participation of all in decision-making.
- Make the goals clear to all.
- Support the followers in accomplishing the objectives and in reaching their potential.

- Discover efficient and economical ways of performing the task.
- Ensure proper and <u>effective communication</u> with the followers. There should be no place for misunderstanding and misinterpretations.
- Be a trainer and not an opponent/critic.

An effective leader is one who meets the job requirements, team requirements as well as individual requirements. While concentrating on the job, a leader would synchronize the departmental goals with the organizational goals. He would ensure that the employees have the required skills and competencies for performing the job effectively and efficiently. He would provide the employees the essential resources for performing the job such as time, knowledge and equipment. He would ensure that employees have no difficulty in performing the tasks assigned to them. And finally, an effective leader would review progress and give the employees a feedback of their performance.

When a leader is focusing on people, he must be compassionate and empathic. He should listen to the employees with understanding. He must respect their views and ideas. He must train and coach them and make an effort to eliminate unnecessary obstacles from the employees' work responsibilities.

Finally, when an effective leader focuses on team, he should coordinate team's efforts. He must celebrate team's success. He should review and promote friendly and social environment. He should develop a team spirit and achievement sense among the employees as a team.

Effective Leadership Skills - What it takes to be an Effective Leader

Who is a leader - A strong leader is one who thinks and plans ahead. He is ready with solutions and he understands the pulse of his employees. However, what are the skills which a leader must possess to be able to do his job well?

Read on to know how even YOU can be an effective leader...

Master Your Time: Effective leaders will always be in a position to manage their time well. They would know how to prioritize list of activities / pending tasks. Most important - they would know the different between 'urgent' and 'important'. Remember, not everything that is urgent is important. Also, not everything that is important is urgent.

Ask Questions: Leaders will ask questions that help them assess employees' contribution to the organization and also help employees understand how better they can contribute towards organizational goals. A Leader must ask his / her employees - the task they perform, do they feel their task is linked to the big picture, and is there anything that comes in the way of their performance.

Provide Work-Life Balance: In today's world where working hours are on a rise, an effective leader must ensure that his / her workers are able to maintain a balance between their personal and professional lives. Effective leaders should always lead by example by leaving on time, avoiding meetings during Fridays or end of the business days, not calling employees on their day off. Remember, an effective leader will have effective followers only if they are not burnt out or feel they are over worked.

Manage Employee's Professional growth: An effective leader will always chart out a personal development plan [PDP] along with his / her employee. He would identify the training the employee will need to go through keeping in mind his personal development plan. The employees will feel encouraged and valued.

Let your employees speak: An effective leader has to be a good listener. Have an "open hour" with your employees and let them speak their heart out. You will be surprised to know the number of ideas they have. Always follow and believe in the mantra "Silence is Golden". Your employees will feel they are being heard and they also have a way to express their thoughts.

Facilitate Brainstorming... Generate ideas: Effective leaders will always encourage people to get together in a room and brainstorm on ideas to solve a particular problem. Remember, discussions are always healthy and almost all the times they also help creating solutions which are mutually agreed upon.

Create Talent Pool: Smart leaders will always be ready for any shortage in staff. They will have their talent pool ready in case of any crisis situation. They will ensure that every employee has a trained / trainable back-up.

Be Courageous: As per Peter Drucker, "whenever you see a successful business, someone once made a courageous decision". An effective leader will always be ready to take difficult / courageous decisions when required.

Be Competent: The art of "tooting your own horn without blowing it" is a delicate balance of demonstrating your "expertise" and "taking credit" in a way that people notice their success. And one of the safest ways to do it is to celebrate and bring attention to team achievements. Praise people for good work, and when you do so, be specific on what exactly you liked. Shaking hands is a gesture that will show them that you are actually happy about their contribution and their success. And thus, you will prove out your competence as a leader.

Be Visionary: What's lying ahead in future is a topic of fascination and has mystic charm. This is a trait of absolute confidence and should be handled with care. It is important to make goals specific, with possible outcomes and benefits, without making promises that you may not be able to keep. A successful leader knows his goals and checks if performance and goals are in symmetry.

Leadership Vision

True leaders have a vision, that is, they have a potential to view the present as it is and to invent a future culminating out of the present. A leader with a vision can foresee the future and can remain in the present. A vision is an end towards which leader can spend and direct his energy and resources. Leaders share a dream and a path which the employees want to share and follow. Leadership vision is not restricted to organizational written mission statement and vision statement. It is well demonstrated in the actions, beliefs and values of organizational leaders.

"If there is no vision, people cannot survive." This is applicable both in business as well in life. Leaders who lack vision cannot succeed in life and they work in a standard and monotonous manner. Vision is not a fantasy for leaders; rather it is a truth that has yet to come into practice. So as to achieve vision, a leader must exert special extra efforts and have robust confidence and devotion to realize the vision. Vision acts as an internal force propelling a leader to act. It provides a leader an objective. The consistent existence of a vision makes a leader progressive despite various hardships and obstacles. Vision is a bond that unites the individuals into team with a mutual goal.

Recognition of a leader's vision by the organizational employees is very essential as it makes the employees well aware of what the organization is trying to achieve. Vision has the strength to move the employees out of monotonous work life and to place them into a new challenging and dynamic work. Vision must be:

- Rational
- Reasonable
- Innovative
- Credible
- Clear
- Motivating and stimulating
- Challenging
- Reflective of organizational beliefs, values and culture
- Concrete

It is a leader who moulds, interprets, communicates and represents the vision. Vision is a portrait and depiction of what a leader aspires his organization to be in long-term.

Different Types of Power

Power has been an important aspect of human civilization since time immemorial. Power might be physical, political or social. In the context of business as well, power dynamics tend to influence decisions and people transactions heavily. So defining power can be difficult as it is understood and interpreted in several ways however power can definitely not be called a force which gets you what you want. Power basically emanates from position or authority which can influence people both positively and negatively.

For simplicity and understanding purposes power is usually classified into following categories:

1. **Coercive Power-** This kind of power involves the usage of threat to make people do what one desires. In the organizational set up, it translates into threatening someone with transfer, firing, demotions etc. it basically forces people to submit to one's demand for the fear of losing something.

2. **Reward Power-** As the name suggests, this type of power uses rewards, perks, new projects or training opportunities, better roles and monetary benefits to influence people. However an interesting aspect of this type of power is that, it is not powerful enough in itself, as decisions related to rewards do not rest solely with the

person promising them, because in organizations, a lot of other people come into play like senior managers and board.

3. **Legitimate Power-** This power emanates from an official position held by someone, be it in an organization, beurocracy or government etc. The duration of this power is short lived as a person can use it only till the time he/she holds that position, as well as, the scope of the power is small as it is strictly defined by the position held.

4. **Expert Power-** This is a personal kind of power which owes its genesis to the skills and expertise possessed by an individual, which is of higher quality and not easily available. In such a situation, the person can exercise the power of knowledge to influence people. Since, it is very person specific and skills can be enhanced with time; it has more credibility and respect.

5. **Referent Power-** This is a power wielded by celebrities and film stars as they have huge following amongst masses who like them, identify with them and follow them. Hence, they exert lasting influence on a large number of people for a large number of decisions; like from what car to buy to which candidate to choose for a higher office in the country.

So, power can be defined in a number of ways however what is important is the usage of the power by people who possess it. Within the organizational context the power dynamics and equations need to be carefully managed as they have a huge impact on the motivation and engagement level of employees. It also defines the organization's culture in general and people transactions within the organization in particular. A very hierarchy and power driven organization finds it difficult to accommodate new and innovative ideas, any change is vehemently refused, egos clash and lesser opportunities are made available for the high performers, thus delaying organizational growth. On the other hand, in an organization which is flat in structure, people are encouraged to innovate and explore, thus bringing in new concepts and ideas to accelerate organizational growth and expansion.

References

www.google.com

www.wikipedia.com

www.managementebooks.com

www.bookboon.com

www.managementbooks.com